I Never Thought It Would Be Like This

A Play

Evelyn Hood

Samuel French - London
New York - Sydney - Toronto - Hollywood

Copyright © 1982 by Evelyn Hood
All Rights Reserved

I NEVER THOUGHT IT WOULD BE LIKE THIS is fully protected under the copyright laws of the British Commonwealth, including Canada, the United States of America, and all other countries of the Copyright Union. All rights, including professional and amateur stage productions, recitation, lecturing, public reading, motion picture, radio broadcasting, television and the rights of translation into foreign languages are strictly reserved.

ISBN 978-0-573-12113-5

www.samuelfrench.co.uk
www.samuelfrench.com

FOR AMATEUR PRODUCTION ENQUIRIES

UNITED KINGDOM AND WORLD EXCLUDING NORTH AMERICA

plays@SamuelFrench-London.co.uk

020 7255 4302/01

Each title is subject to availability from Samuel French,
depending upon country of performance.

CAUTION: Professional and amateur producers are hereby warned that I NEVER THOUGHT IT WOULD BE LIKE THIS is subject to a licensing fee. Publication of this play does not imply availability for performance. Both amateurs and professionals considering a production are strongly advised to apply to the appropriate agent before starting rehearsals, advertising, or booking a theatre. A licensing fee must be paid whether the title is presented for charity or gain and whether or not admission is charged.

The professional rights in this play are controlled by Pollinger Ltd, Staple Inn, London WC1V 7QH

No one shall make any changes in this title for the purpose of production. No part of this book may be reproduced, stored in a retrieval system, or transmitted in any form, by any means, now known or yet to be invented, including mechanical, electronic, photocopying, recording, videotaping, or otherwise, without the prior written permission of the publisher. No one shall upload this title, or part of this title, to any social media websites.

The right of Evelyn Hood to be identified as author of this work has been asserted in accordance with Section 77 of the Copyright, Designs and Patents Act 1988.

I Never Thought It Would Be Like This

Characters—

Doreen
Arthur
Mum
Norman

The action takes place on a tropical desert island

Time—the present

I NEVER THOUGHT IT WOULD BE LIKE THIS

A clearing on a tropical island

There are a few rocks or fallen trees, sand, possibly a glimpse of sea between the trees

Doreen and Arthur have just arrived, and are looking round. She is a very ordinary person, wearing a slightly crumpled floral dress. She carries a large knitting bag. She is the sort of person determined to make the best out of any situation she finds herself in. Life must be familiar at all times. Arthur is looking about like a prospective house-buyer sizing up the property. He likes to think that he is always in charge of the situation

Doreen Oh, this looks nice. Shall we sit here for a minute?
Arthur Might as well. We've seen most of the island by now.

They sit on rocks, or a fallen tree. Doreen delves into her bag and produces some bright pink knitting. She starts working on it as though her life depends on it

Doreen Well, at least the weather cleared up.
Arthur Yes.
Doreen When I woke up this morning, down there on the beach, I thought, thank goodness that gale's gone down.
Arthur (*looking around thoughtfully*) Yes.
Doreen I mean, you don't expect storms on a nice summer cruise, do you? Not when they advertised it as a sparkling sunshine cruise.
Arthur (*with sudden dislike*) Do you have to knit all the time? You knitted on the ship, you knitted in the lifeboat, and you're still knitting.
Doreen It keeps my hands busy. Always keep your hands busy, my mum says.
Arthur Not a sign of anyone.
Doreen I expect they've found somewhere else to land. We'll meet up with them sooner or later.
Arthur I must say, you're taking this very calmly, Miss ...?
Doreen Doreen. Just call me Doreen. When you've been ship-

wrecked with someone you should be friendly, shouldn't you? It makes for a sort of bond. And you're ...?
Arthur Barlow. Arthur Barlow.
Doreen On your own, were you?
Arthur Yes.
Doreen That's nice. Nice that two people on their own should get together like this, I mean. Oh, isn't the sea lovely? All shiny and sparkly.
Arthur And all round us. I feel like a character in a cartoon.
Doreen Pardon?
Arthur Those desert island cartoons.
Doreen Oh, yes. Who'd have thought we'd find ourselves here? Now, what can we do to pass the time?
Arthur (*looking at her as though she is mad*) Well, we'll have to make plans. Plenty of fresh water here, and I expect those nuts and berries will be edible. I wonder if there are any animals I could trap ...
Doreen What about a nice cup of tea?
Arthur I beg your pardon?
Doreen Tea—and a biscuit, of course. Fancy it?
Arthur My dear Miss—Doreen—we are marooned on a desert island. We do not have nice cups of tea and biscuits.
Doreen I do. (*She produces a flask and a plastic cup from her knitting bag, as well as biscuits in a paper napkin*)
Arthur Good heavens!
Doreen I'll be mother, shall I? (*She pours tea into the cup*)
Arthur But—where did you get it?
Doreen (*handing him the cup and pouring tea into the flask top for herself*) My cabin steward left it for me. He knows I get peckish at night. Oh, there's no sugar—is that all right?
Arthur (*dazed*) Quite all right.
Doreen Have a biscuit. Well, the ship sank before I got a chance to feel peckish last night. I grabbed my knitting bag, because I promised mum I'd get this jumper finished for her no matter what. Then I decided to take the tea so that I'd have something to drink in the lifeboat. (*She tastes the tea*) Oh, that's good—it's still warm. Well, in the excitement of the lifeboat sinking just as we got here, I forgot my tea.
Arthur I thought I'd never taste tea again!
Doreen Now there's no need to think like that. You let yourself get into a bit of a state, didn't you?
Arthur Not at all!

I Never Thought It Would Be Like This

Doreen Oh, you can be honest with me. I knew you were getting fussed when you began to pray in the lifeboat.

Arthur You were praying too. I saw your lips move.

Doreen I was praying for a bit of land. You weren't doing either of us much good with "Now I Lay Me Down to Sleep".

Arthur (*huffily*) It was all I could think of under the circumstances.

Doreen Have some more tea. (*She tops up both cups*) If you're going to ask for help, my mum says, ask for something sensible. He's a busy person up there. Anyway, mine worked—we got to land.

Arthur In a way.

Doreen Well, I didn't ask for something with a bingo hall and a couple of hotels on it. I just wanted something solid under my feet instead of all that water sloshing about in the lifeboat. This'll do for the moment.

Arthur I just wish the lifeboat hadn't sprung a leak. We could have done with it.

Doreen *You* certainly could. Lucky I had my knitting bag with me, wasn't it? If I hadn't towed you in with it we might both have been drowned. Honestly, I didn't know what to think when you started to clutch at me like that! The last thing Mum said to me when I was going on this cruise was, take your knitting bag, Doreen, you'll be glad of it. And I was!

Arthur Your mum says quite a lot, doesn't she? (*He wanders round, spying out the land*)

Doreen Oh yes, a tower of strength, my mum. A girl needs a good mum behind her, that's what I was taught. And it's true. When I got the chance of the supermarket job, it was Mum who said, take it, Doreen, and I did. And it's been very secure, just like Mum said. What do you do?

Arthur I'm an administrator.

Doreen (*impressed*) Oh, nice. I work on the fish counter. My friend Beryl, she works on the fish counter too. That tea was nice. I think I'll sunbathe now.

Arthur You can sunbathe later. At the moment we should think of building some sort of shelter.

Doreen Oh, that tree's shelter enough for me. I came on this cruise to get a tan, so I don't want to sit in the shade. I think I'll stretch out on the beach down there for an hour ...

Arthur I'm talking about a shelter we can use during the night.

Doreen During the night? Oh, we won't be here as long as that!

Arthur And how do we get off the island before tonight?

Doreen There'll be another ship along soon.
Arthur (*getting irritated*) This isn't the High Street, you know. Number Ten liners don't come by every half-hour. It could be weeks before we're found, don't you realize that?
Doreen Weeks? I can't stay here for weeks! I'm due back on the fish counter on Monday, and Mr Paterson's very strict. If I'm not back by nine o'clock at the latest on Monday morning I get an hour docked off my wages. If I'm off for three days without a doctor's note I lose my job. I've got to be back for Monday!
Arthur Look, you can just forget about Mr Paterson and the fish counter and ...
Doreen Forget? I can't just forget about them! Twelve years I've worked in that shop. I'm the fish counter supervisor now. Last month I even went to the fish market with Mr Paterson ...
Arthur (*getting hysterical*) Will you shut up about ...
Doreen Doreen knows her fish, he said. 'She's got a good eye for cod. And I have – I got the best cod at bargain prices. He's going to take me again when I get back and ...
Arthur (*plucking her from the rock she is sitting on and shaking her*) Will you shut up about the fish counter and pull yourself together!
Doreen You're – you're crushing my wool.

With a great effort, Arthur calms down and releases her. She backs off, watching him warily

Arthur I'm sorry. I—I don't know what came over me ...
Doreen Yes—well—I'll have to have a think about this.
Arthur We'll just have to make the best of the situation.
Doreen I don't know what Mum's going to say. I'm supposed to be home in time to help her hang the new curtains.
Arthur You are not going to be there to hang the new curtains. We're marooned, cast ashore, high and dry ...
Doreen (*shouting at him irritably*) Well, do something about it! You're a man, aren't you? Men are supposed to know how to cope with this sort of thing, aren't they? So go ahead and cope with it! (*She starts to knit furiously again*)
Arthur That's what I'm trying to do!
Doreen Do it, then!
Arthur Right! First we assess the situation, which is ...
Doreen That I have to be back at the fish counter first thing on Monday.

I Never Thought It Would Be Like This

Arthur (*ignoring her*) That we are stuck here, just the two of us. Right?
Doreen Well, it doesn't take much brain to see that there's just the two of us.
Arthur It's a matter of establishing a workable routine, that's all. How are you on woodland lore?
Doreen Pardon?
Arthur Were you ever a Girl Guide?
Doreen I went once, but we ate some stuff round the camp fire and I was sick so I didn't go back.
Arthur Have you ever gone camping?
Doreen Me and Mum went in a luxury caravan once. Only it rained all the time and I fell down the steps and broke my ankle.
Arthur Any hobbies that might be of use?

Mutely, she holds out her knitting

No, none. Work—you're on the fish counter. Well, we'll have to eat a lot of fish.
Doreen I only sell them—I wouldn't know how to catch them or clean them. They come to me after they're dead.
Arthur So all we have to do is to catch some filleted fish and find someone you can sell them to.
Doreen (*hurt*) I'm a very good salesgirl. I even won the Salton's Super Salesperson prize. I won this rotten cruise, that's what I won. And I wish I'd come in second! (*She is on the verge of tears*)
Arthur (*hurriedly*) Don't get upset, Miss—er—Doreen. I'm sure you're an excellent salesgirl. But we don't need salesgirls, do we? We need—just about everything else.
Doreen Well, what do you do? An administrator, you said. What did you administer?

Arthur hesitates, then mutters something

I didn't hear that.
Arthur I said I worked for a funeral parlour.
Doreen You mean, an undertaker?
Arthur A funeral parlour!

She squeals, jumps up, backs away from him

Well, someone has to do it! I'm sick of all this fuss every time I tell someone what I do!
Doreen A date with death!
Arthur A what?
Doreen A date with death! Mum saw it in the tea leaves the very

night before I sailed. A ship and water, and a date with death. That's you!

Arthur Don't talk rubbish! I'm very much alive, and so are you.

Doreen And I'm going to stay that way, so don't you get any funny ideas!

Arthur I bury people, I don't kill them! Nobody accuses you of murdering your damned supermarket fish, do they?

Doreen Don't you shout at me!

Arthur *I'm not shouting!*

Doreen begins to sniffle into her knitting

(*Quickly*) Don't cry—you can't afford to lose the salt.

Doreen I should have stayed at home. I'm going to grow old here, and die here—and you'll be glad because you'll be able to arrange my funeral, won't you?

Arthur No I won't. Look, I don't want to stay here either. I'm trying to think of something.

Doreen Build a fire so that ships can see it.

Arthur It'd take days to collect enough wood.

Doreen Well—climb that tree over there and look for ships.

Arthur They're not likely to see me sitting at the top of a tree, are they? They'll be miles away, on the horizon.

Doreen Wave something!

Arthur What?

Doreen Well—er—(*she looks down at herself*)—I haven't got anything you can use. Take your shirt off, that'll do. (*She flies at him and tries to drag his shirt off*) Go on, get up there and wave your shirt until someone comes.

Arthur (*fighting her off*) It could take weeks!

Doreen You aren't doing anything else, are you?

Arthur Besides, you can't climb a palm tree unaided. The islanders use ropes, and sharp things on their feet.

Doreen You can use my knitting needles when I've finished this bit, if you're quick with them.

Arthur I am not climbing a palm tree with knitting needles, and that's final!

Doreen Build a boat.

Arthur I will—when I've found out how to cut down trees and shape the wood. Not to mention making a sail.

Doreen A plane might come over.

Arthur There hasn't been one so far.

Doreen You're not trying!

Arthur You're not giving me a chance! I tell you what. I'll swim out there and I'll catch a cod and bring it back. You can explain the situation to it, then I'll let it go. And when it meets up with Mr Paterson in the fish market next Monday at nine o'clock prompt, it can bloody well tell him where you are!

Doreen glares at him, then slowly sits down and starts knitting

That's better. Now I'm going to build a shelter for tonight.
Doreen Two shelters.
Arthur (*stopping on his way out of the clearing and turning*) Did you say something?
Doreen I am certainly not going to share a shelter with a man I only met a few hours ago in a lifeboat.
Arthur Oh yes, you are. We're living under island law now, don't you forget that.
Doreen Are you married?
Arthur Well, yes, but ...
Doreen And you have the nerve to blatantly proposition me behind your poor wife's back?
Arthur Constance is thousands of miles away. (*Struck by a pleasant thought*) I may never see her again ...
Doreen The next thing you're going to say is that she doesn't understand you anyway, isn't it?
Arthur Now, just a minute ...
Doreen I couldn't be a party to such deceit. I couldn't do it and look my mum in the face.
Arthur Look, let's leave your mum out of it for a start. She's out of your life now.
Doreen Oh no she's not. My Mum's very important to me. I wouldn't do anything without talking it over with Mum first.
Arthur I could have been ship-wrecked with Jane Fonda or Olivia Newton John. Why do I have to get landed with a mother-complex?
Doreen I didn't ask you to come in my lifeboat, did I? I didn't ask you to grab hold of my knitting bag when you were drowning. No need to go insulting Mum like that. A girl needs her mum behind her.
Mum That's right, Doreen, you tell him!

Arthur turns, and gapes. Mum, an older version of Doreen, is sitting on an ordinary fireside chair in the clearing, knitting something virulent green. Doreen goes on knitting calmly

Arthur Wh—what's she doing here?
Doreen I told you, I don't feel right without Mum.
Arthur Get rid of her!
Doreen What do you mean, get rid of her? That's my Mum you're talking about!
Arthur But she's not really here.
Doreen Don't call people "she", it's rude.
Mum That's right.
Arthur She's a figment of your imagination, that's all. She's only here because you won't put her out of your mind. She's really at home...
Mum Watching telly. But it wasn't a very good film anyway, love.
Arthur You see? She *is* a figment of your imagination.
Doreen Oh, I know that.
Arthur So all you have to do is stop thinking about her, and she'll vanish.
Doreen Oh, I couldn't do that to Mum.
Arthur Yes, you could. Go on—stop thinking about her.
Doreen But I wouldn't know how to stop thinking about Mum. Besides, if she's here it's because I want her to be here, isn't that right?
Mum That's right, love.
Doreen And if I want her here, I wouldn't want to send her away again, would I?
Mum No, you wouldn't, love.
Arthur Doreen! All right, then, I'll think up Constance. How would you like *that*?
Doreen That'd be nice. You'd like to meet Constance, wouldn't you, Mum?
Mum What's she like?
Doreen Oh, she'll be a nice person.
Arthur Constance is not a nice person.
Doreen I expect we'll like her.
Arthur Very well, then...

He concentrates hard. Doreen and Mum watch expectantly. Nothing happens. Arthur moves away from the women, tries again

Doreen P'raps she's taken the phone off the hook.
Mum Doesn't seem to want to know, does she?
Arthur (*hissing into the trees*) Constance! Constance?
Doreen P'raps she's busy thinking about something else.

Arthur Shopping, that's what she's doing! Out spending my money! Women!
Mum It's a knack our Doreen has. You have to be really fond of someone before it works.
Arthur I didn't really want her here anyway.
Doreen His wife doesn't understand him.
Mum They never do.
Arthur Right. I'll leave Constance where she is, if you get rid of your mother.
Mum So it's come to that, has it? I'm not wanted in my own daughter's life!
Arthur Just let your mind go blank for a moment, and she'll go.
Doreen Oh no, she won't. You don't know my mum.
Arthur I don't want to!
Mum You're going to have to!
Arthur Doreen, you're going to have to make a choice—her or me.
Mum A girl needs a good mum behind her.
Doreen A girl needs a good mum behind her.
Arthur Doreen, just think about it. We're facing a new life together. The world's our oyster.
Doreen You just want me to share that shelter with you, don't you?
Arthur I just want you to realize that there's a whole new future here.
Doreen What about your wife?
Arthur Forget her.
Doreen But we wouldn't be married.
Arthur Marriage belongs to the old way of life.
Doreen Being married would be nice.
Arthur We will be, in our own way.
Mum Huh!
Doreen What if you went off with someone else when I was old and worn out, and deserted me?
Arthur Who else could I go off with?
Doreen Well—there might be another ship-wreck, and a beautiful girl might come from the sea, like in a film, and you'd go off with her, wouldn't you?
Arthur I wouldn't!
Mum Oh yes he would.
Doreen Oh yes, I know you would. And leave me alone, tired out from looking after the kids, nothing to look forward to . . .
Arthur Either she goes, or I will!

Doreen Where would you go?
Arthur I'll find somewhere!
Doreen Go on then.
Arthur Right—I will!

Arthur storms off into the trees. The women knit in silence for a moment

Doreen Isn't it lovely and quiet here?
Mum Mmm. Wouldn't mind a choc-ice, though.

A brief cry of pain is heard. They ignore it

Doreen Oh, yes! I wish you hadn't made me think about a choc-ice, Mum.

Arthur limps in, sits down, stares straight ahead

Arthur I used to dream about being cast away on an island. I imagined the water sparkling, the white sand warm beneath my feet.
Mum You can tell he's a reader, Doreen.
Arthur Somehow, I never thought it would be like this.
Doreen I remember the first time I saw Blackpool Tower in the flesh, so to speak. I was ever so disappointed.
Arthur I thought, when we landed here, that it would be a new start for me. I'd manage things, and you'd look up to me. But I've changed, somehow.
Doreen People change.
Arthur You haven't.
Doreen Some people don't change.
Arthur I came back.
Doreen Yes, I can see that. Did you forget something?
Arthur There was nowhere to go.
Doreen There never is, not really.
Arthur This is it. The place where we have to stop and face up to things.
Doreen All I've got to face up to is what Mr Paterson's going to say if I don't turn up on Monday. And there's Mum—but her memory's a comfort.
Arthur I always wanted to be important. I thought I might be important here—to you. But I can't climb a palm tree, I can't open coconuts with my teeth, I can't get help—I'm nothing to write home about, am I?
Doreen Even if you were we couldn't write home about you, could

we? Not unless we put the letter in the vacuum flask and floated it. I wonder if it would? You never hear of notes in flasks, do you? Or ships in flasks.

Arthur (*sadly*) You couldn't see a ship in a flask.

Doreen I expect that's why. And you can't keep tomato soup warm in a bottle, can you?

Arthur I banged my leg on a rock back there.

Doreen It'll get better. Come on, cheer up.

Arthur It's just a touch of depression. I'll get over it in a few days— or a few weeks.

Doreen, concerned, goes over to Mum and they argue in whispers. Then Doreen goes to Arthur and touches his shoulder

Doreen All right—I'll share your shelter with you.

Arthur But what about...?

Doreen Well, she's not very pleased, but she'll have to lump it. After all, I refused Tom Irvine because she didn't like his ears. I can't give in to her every time.

Mum Tom Irvine turned out to have a wife and two kids in Newcastle.

Doreen We won't talk about that, if you don't mind.

Arthur (*his confidence restored*) Well, that's settled, then! I'll go and start work on that shelter, shall I?

Arthur and Doreen start to get a bit coy with each other

Doreen Yes, I suppose you'd better.

Arthur Oh yes. It gets cold in these tropical places at night.

Doreen I could rip this out and knit you a nice sweater, if you like.

Mum sighs heavily

Arthur Oh, I couldn't deprive your mum...

Doreen She can easily knit one for herself, can't you, Mum?

Mum grunts

Besides, I can hardly send it to her in the flask, can I?

Arthur I suppose not. Well, I'd best get on with that shelter, then.

Doreen Want any help?

Arthur (*in control of the situation again*) I should manage. I turned my hand to a fair bit of do-it-yourself at home.

Doreen (*impressed*) Oh? I can't do anything—except knitting, of course.

Arthur I finished a cocktail cabinet for Constance just before the cruise, as a matter of fact.
Doreen Fancy! Furniture's a terrible price, isn't it? Making it yourself helps when you've got a wife and family to support.
Arthur Just a wife. No children.
Mum Why not?
Arthur Well, Constance doesn't really care for ... Doreen, could you please stop thinking about your mother, even for a little while?
Doreen But if I let her go, I might not be able to get her back again.
Arthur Why don't you try it?
Mum Too late for that. I've made up my mind to stop until I'm satisfied.
Arthur About what?
Mum Your intentions.
Doreen Mum's right, Arthur. This is a serious step I'm taking. I have to be sure I'm choosing the right partner.
Arthur You're choosing the only partner! I'm the only man within a thousand miles!
Mum Sad, isn't it?
Doreen I've still got the right to know all about you, haven't I? And things like where we're going to settle down.
Arthur We're going to settle down in a little shelter over there, aren't we?
Doreen Well, I suppose it's quite a nice area. But I'd always fancied a nice house near Mum, then we could pop in on each other during the day.
Mum What about future prospects?
Arthur From what I can gather—not too rosy.
Doreen What about a family?
Arthur What about it?
Doreen I'd want children.
Arthur All right, we'll have children.
Doreen At least one of each.
Arthur Fine.
Doreen How many do you want?
Arthur I haven't had much time to think about it.
Doreen You'd like a son, wouldn't you, Arthur?
Arthur A son? Come to think of it, I wouldn't mind a son. Arthur Barlow, junior.
Doreen Oh no—Norman.
Arthur Who?

I Never Thought It Would Be Like This

Mum Norman.
Arthur Not Norman.
Doreen Why not Norman?
Arthur I—I knew a Norman once. I didn't like him.
Doreen You'll like this one. He's going to be very well behaved, and nice, and he's going to be a brain surgeon.
Arthur He was a bully. Grew up to be an all-in wrestler.
Doreen My Norman won't be a bully.
Arthur He's going to be a *what*?
Doreen A brain surgeon.
Arthur How can he be a brain surgeon if we're stuck on this island?
Doreen I've set my heart on it.
Arthur He'll be a boat-builder, or a fisherman.
Doreen Not Norman.
Norman Not me!

Arthur spins round. Norman, a young man, is sitting on a rock

I'd rather be a brain surgeon.
Doreen Your dad says you've got to be a fisherman.
Arthur You've been thinking about Norman too, haven't you?
Doreen (*Dreamily*) For years and years.
Norman Why can't I be a brain surgeon?
Doreen Why can't he be Norman, for a start? Oh, your father's being very difficult, Norman. I do hope you aren't going to grow up like him. I've had such a day with him, you wouldn't imagine...
Mum That was her dad's name—Norman.
Arthur Then it's right out. I don't hold with calling children after relatives. It only means you have to go on and on having children until all the names have been used up.
Mum By the look of things, you won't be doing anything else anyway, will you?
Doreen I like Norman for a name. And Norman likes Norman for a name, don't you, Norman?
Arthur What's wrong with—(*he searches for a name, finds one*)—Richard?
Doreen What's wrong with Richard is that it's not Norman.
Arthur But I like it.
Doreen Norman Richard, then.
Arthur Richard Norman.
Doreen Suit yourself. I'll call him Norman.
Arthur And I'll call him Richard.

Norman And I won't know whether I'm coming or going. Make up your minds, can't you?
Arthur Toss a coin.
Doreen Certainly not. Are you going to call that boy after my father, or are you not?
Arthur I don't see why I should.
Doreen Then there's nothing left to say, is there?
Norman I'd like to say ...
Doreen Oh—shut up!

Silence while she sulks, Arthur watches her warily, and Mum knits

Arthur Well—I'd best get on with that shelter, then.
Doreen *Two* shelters!
Arthur I beg your pardon?
Doreen If we're going to quarrel like this, and if you're going to insist on having your own way all the time—I'd like my own shelter, please.
Arthur Oh—bloody hell! (*He sits on a rock, furious*)
Norman Who's this?
Mum I'm your grandma.
Norman D'you live here too?
Mum Only in a manner of speaking. I'm tolerated and no more.
Arthur Oh, all right then—Norman.
Doreen (*knitting busily, still cool with him*) Thank you.
Arthur And now I'm going to build that blasted shelter before you change your mind again.
Norman Hey—what about me?
Doreen What about you?
Norman What's going to happen to me?
Arthur That's a stupid question.
Doreen Yes, it is. I'm surprised at you, Norman.
Arthur You'll be born, like anyone else, and you'll grow up, that's what'll happen to you. Take things as they come, that's what your mother and me always had to do.
Norman But I want to be a brain surgeon!
Arthur Honestly, kids nowadays are spoiled rotten. Nobody bothered to ask me what I'd like to be before I was born.
Norman But it was different for you! How can I learn to be a brain surgeon here? Experiment on coconuts?
Doreen He's right, Arthur.
Arthur We'll get off the island before it's time to worry about that.

Norman But there's my early education to consider. You can't just neglect that, you know.
Doreen We'll take care of it, won't we, Arthur?
Arthur Well—I know a bit of French, and I was quite good at maths at school. I can teach him how to make things too.
Doreen There, you see? And I'll teach you to cook and to knit. Knitting's good for your hands, and you have to have good hands to become a brain surgeon. I'll teach you a bit of singing too. I used to be in the chorus at the local operatic club.
Norman Fat lot of good that'll be to someone who wants to study brain surgery!
Doreen Don't answer your mother back!
Arthur I'll teach him to fish, and to swim.
Doreen Didn't see much sign of you swimming when I towed you ashore with my knitting bag.
Arthur I was stunned then. I happen to swim very well.
Norman Why can't I have a father who can teach me useful things?
Doreen Yes—why can't he have a father who can teach him useful things?
Arthur Because I'm an administrator, that's why!
Doreen Burying people isn't going to get him very far, is it? I'm beginning to wonder if this will work out, Arthur. You're not my type, not really.
Arthur Beggars can't be choosers.
Doreen If that remark is aimed at me, let me remind you that I turned down Tom Irvine. I haven't exactly been on the shelf...
Mum She's off again.
Doreen And you can keep quiet, Mum, or I'll stop thinking about you!
Mum Oh no, I'm staying. I've been here long enough to feel quite solid. I can stay by myself now.
Doreen Well, if you're that solid, there's nothing to stop me from pitching you into the water, is there?
Arthur Doreen, that's enough!
Mum Thank you, son.
Arthur Now don't you go thinking that I'm taking your side...
Mum We need each other when she gets on her high horse. Behind every successful husband stands his mother-in-law.
Arthur Doreen...
Doreen Fine partner you turned out to be! There's that poor lad

sitting there, wanting to learn something that'll stand him in good stead later on in life, and what can his father teach him? How to bury people!

Arthur I didn't exactly do that myself! I'm an administrator.

Doreen What's the use of an administrator with nothing to administrate?

Arthur It's no more useless than someone who can sell fish but doesn't know how to fillet the damned things!

Doreen Don't be personal!

Arthur I'd give anything right now to slam a door!

Doreen You'd have to make it first, wouldn't you? And before you do that, you can build a boat for me. I'm leaving!

Norman You can't leave now! What's going to happen to me?

Arthur Doreen, you're taking a very serious step...

Doreen Just build a boat, please!

Arthur Er—I think we should talk about this. I mean, if you walk out on me, I might not take you back later...

Doreen A small boat will do!

Arthur And there's—er—alimony. And there's—er—custody of—er—(*he looks at Mum and Norman*)—Well—I mean—...

Doreen (*slowly*) Tell me about this boat.

Arthur Which boat?

Doreen The one you're going to build to get us off this island.

Arthur It's—er—what can you say about a boat?

Doreen Made of what?

Norman (*helpfully*) Wood?

Arthur Yes—wood!

Doreen And do you know how you're going to build it?

Arthur Well—I thought—that is...

Mum I think you've got him, Doreen.

Doreen You don't know how to build a boat, do you?

Arthur I'll work it out as I go along.

Doreen You're scared to try, aren't you?

Norman Yes, he is!

Arthur (*quickly*) No I'm not!

Mum Not much!

Doreen All we need is something small.

Arthur It's just that...

Norman That what?

Arthur (*miserably*) It would sink.

Doreen Of course it wouldn't.

Mum I bet it would!

Arthur sits down and picks up Doreen's knitting

Arthur (*starting to knit*) It would if I made it. Everything goes wrong with me.
Doreen What about that lovely cocktail cabinet you made?
Arthur I put a full bottle in it, and it collapsed.
Doreen Oh, dear!
Arthur (*wretchedly*) Port all over the carpet. Two glasses from a new set broken.
Doreen What did Constance say?
Arthur She laughed. They all laughed. We were having a party at the time.
Doreen Well, it shows she's got a sense of humour.
Arthur When they'd gone she hit me on the head with the leg of the cocktail cabinet. That's why I went on the cruise. I told her— one of us will have to go, Constance, I said. So here I am.
Norman Look, what are you going to do about my future?
Doreen Oh Norman, stop bothering your poor father! Go away and find something useful to do! (*She shoos Norman out of the clearing*)

Norman goes

Doreen returns to Arthur

She shouldn't have hit you. I wouldn't do that to anyone.
Arthur I don't think you would. You're kinder than she is.
Doreen And we don't need cocktail cabinets, do we? Though I'm sure you'll make a lovely cabinet one day.
Arthur D'you think so?
Doreen All you need's encouragement. And time. We've got plenty of that. With a bit of encouragement I'm sure you could build a beautiful shelter.
Arthur Really?
Doreen And a lovely boat. *You* could do it, Arthur.
Mum All a man needs is a good woman behind him.
Doreen Or two good women.
Mum Even better.

Arthur puts down the knitting, confidence restored

Arthur I don't see why not. I thought we could make the shelter by lashing palm leaves together. A temporary measure, of course. Once I get going I can make a proper hut. What d'you think?
Doreen Lovely.

Arthur We'll need creeper to tie the leaves . . .
Doreen Or wool?
Arthur You'll need that to knit my sweater.
Doreen Oh yes, so I will.
Arthur Creeper, then. I'll go and look for some.
Doreen I'll come and help you.
Arthur Constance would never have offered to help me.

They gaze into each other's eyes

Doreen I know.

Doreen grabs Arthur's hand and they go out of the clearing together

(*As they disappear*) Do you think we could make wool out of creeper?

Mum is left alone, knitting

After a moment Norman comes back

Norman Look, I don't care how you feel about it all, it's my future, and I'm . . . Where are they?
Mum They've gone to build a shelter.
Norman One shelter?
Mum Yes. Romantic, isn't it?
Norman That probably means I'm going to happen whether I want to or not.
Mum Probably.
Norman I'll bet he's a rotten father. I'll bet he won't be able to teach me anything at all.
Mum After they've built the shelter, they're going to build a boat.
Norman (*with interest*) Really?
Mum She's going to stand by him. A man needs a good woman to stand by him, Norman.
Norman Do you think he'll be able to build it? The boat?
Mum No.
Norman Oh.
Mum You see, Norman, every good woman needs her mum behind her before she can stand behind her man. That's why I'm staying.
Norman (*brightening again*) You mean you're going to help them to build the boat properly?
Mum I'm going to try.
Norman Could you try hard, for my sake?
Mum Well, seeing that you're to be named after my dead hubby,

and seeing that you're a nice enough lad—and seeing that those parents of yours couldn't be trusted to bring you up the right way on this island—I'll try hard.
Norman Thanks, Grandma.

She takes a skein of wool from her bag, puts it over his hands so that she can wind it into a ball

Mum Never forget, Norman, that behind every successful brain surgeon stands his granny.
Norman (*thoughtfully*) That's true.

CURTAIN

FURNITURE AND PROPERTY LIST

On stage: Rocks, trees, fallen trees, sand Fireside chair, concealed in shadow. *On it:* green knitting, skein of wool

Off stage: Large bag containing bright pink knitting, flask of tea, plastic cup, biscuits in paper napkin (DOREEN)

LIGHTING PLOT

Property fittings required: nil
Exterior. A tropical island
To open: General effect of hot daylight, with darkened areas to conceal MUM and NORMAN
Cue 1:   MUM: "That's right, Doreen, you tell him!"   (Page 7)
       Bring up lighting on MUM's chair
Cue 2:   NORMAN: "Not me!"   (Page 13)
       Bring up lighting on NORMAN'S rock

www.ingramcontent.com/pod-product-compliance
Ingram Content Group UK Ltd.
Pitfield, Milton Keynes, MK11 3LW, UK
UKHW021849210426
5322IPUK00022B/554